Dear Parent:
Your child's love of reading starts here!

Every child learns to read in a different way and at his or her own speed. Some go back and forth between reading levels and read favorite books again and again. Others read through each level in order. You can help your young reader improve and become more confident by encouraging his or her own interests and abilities. From books your child reads with you to the first books he or she reads alone, there are I Can Read Books for every stage of reading:

SHARED READING
Basic language, word repetition, and whimsical illustrations, ideal for sharing with your emergent reader

BEGINNING READING
Short sentences, familiar words, and simple concepts for children eager to read on their own

READING WITH HELP
Engaging stories, longer sentences, and language play for developing readers

READING ALONE
Complex plots, challenging vocabulary, and high-interest topics for the independent reader

I Can Read Books have introduced children to the joy of reading since 1957. Featuring award-winning authors and illustrators and a fabulous cast of beloved characters, I Can Read Books set the standard for beginning readers.

A lifetime of discovery begins with the magical words **"I Can Read!"**

*Visit www.icanread.com for information
on enriching your child's reading experience.*

**Visit www.zonderkidz.com/icanread for more faith-based
I Can Read! titles from Zonderkidz.**

ZONDERKIDZ

I Can Read Fiona Goes to School
Copyright © 2021 by Zondervan
Illustrations: © 2021 by Zondervan

An **I Can Read Book**

Requests for information should be addressed to:
Zonderkidz, 3900 *Sparks Drive SE, Grand Rapids, Michigan 49546*

Softcover ISBN 978-0-310-75483-1
Hardcover ISBN 978-0-310-75496-1
Ebook ISBN 978-0-310-75507-4

Zonderkidz is a trademark of Zondervan.

Art direction and design: Diane Mielke
Content Contributor: Barbara Herndon

I Can Read® and I Can Read Book® are trademarks of HarperCollins Publishers.

Printed in United States of America

22 23 24 25 26 27 /LSCC/ 15 14 13 12 11 10 9 8 7 6 5 4 3 2 1

ZONDER**kidz**™ · BEGINNING READING 1 · I Can Read!

Fiona
Goes to School

New York Times **Bestselling Illustrator**
Richard Cowdrey
with Donald Wu

ZONDER**kidz**

It was a busy day at the zoo.

Boys and girls waved
to Fiona and Mama in the pool.

"There are so many boys and
girls here today," said Fiona.
"Where did they come from?"

Mama said, "The kids are on
a school trip."
"What is school?" Fiona asked.

"School is a place to learn
new things.
Schools have friends, teachers,
and lots of books," said Mama.

8

Fiona liked to learn new things.

She liked friends.

She liked books too.

"I want to go to school!"

shouted Fiona.

Fiona went for a walk around
the zoo.

She went to see her friends.

Giraffe, Kris the cheetah,
and the monkeys walked with Fiona.

People were leaving the zoo.
The animals saw many big,
yellow buses in the parking lot.
They were filled with laughing kids

"What are those?" asked the
monkeys. "They are school buses.
They take kids to school and the
zoo," said Giraffe.

13

School sounded fun. Buses looked
fun. "I wish there was a zoo
school," said Fiona.

"A zoo school?" Giraffe said.

"I want to go to zoo school."

"Me too!" said Kris.

"Let's start our own zoo school,"
shouted Fiona.

Soon the zoo school was ready.

Mr. Elephant was very smart.

He was the school teacher.

He called out, "Good morning!

Let's start school."

All the animals were happy.

They wanted to learn.

They wanted to have fun.

They wanted Mr. Elephant to
read to them too.

"We are going to learn about elephants," Mr. Elephant said. "Elephants are the best animal. They are very smart and big," he started.

"What about snakes?" hissed Snake.

"What about lakes?" asked Otter.

Fiona wanted Mr. Elephant to
read a book.

All the zoo school students were
squawking, peeping, and chattering.
It was loud!

Mr. Barn Owl flew to the school.

"Whoooo is so loud?" he hooted.

"Zoo school students should
listen to the teacher," Owl said.

Mr. Owl had an idea.

He talked to Mr. Elephant.

Then he hooted,
"Today, I will teach you
about school.
Tomorrow, Mr. Elephant will
be the teacher again."

So Mr. Barn Owl told the animals
about being good listeners.
And about raising their
paws, flipper, or hooves to talk.

24

Mr. Barn Owl talked about respect.

And about sharing and naptime!

"What about snakes?" hissed Snake.

"What about lakes?" asked Otter.

Fiona still wanted a book.

Then Fiona had an idea.

Fiona raised a leg and said,

"I've got this! Let's have a new

teacher every day!"

So the next day,
Mr. Elephant
taught about elephants.

And the next day,
Mrs. Snake
hissed all about snakes.

27

On the next day of zoo school
the class had fun learning about
lakes from Mr. and Mrs. Otter.

And on the last day of zoo school
Fiona's Mama came and read a book
The zoo school students loved
reading books!

"Thank you for reading to us!"
they all said when Mama was
finished.

"I love school," Fiona
said to Mama
as they walked home.
"I knew you would!"